To Nessie
Wishing you a [...] [...]
and a happy [...] [...].
Best wishes
Howard
Dec 2012

a year in the life of wimbledon joanna jackson

a year in the life of wimbledon joanna jackson

F

FRANCES LINCOLN LIMITED
PUBLISHERS

To Ben and Jake,
May all your dreams come true

Frances Lincoln Ltd
4 Torriano Mews
Torriano Avenue
London NW5 2RZ
www.franceslincoln.com

A Year in the Life of Wimbledon
Copyright © Frances Lincoln Limited 2012
Text and photographs copyright ©
Joanna Jackson 2012
First Frances Lincoln edition 2012

A catalogue record for this book is available
from the British Library.

ISBN: 9780711232662

Printed and bound in China

9 8 7 6 5 4 3 2 1

OPPOSITE: Wimbledon Common
and Windmill
PAGE1: The New Wimbledon Theatre
at night
PAGES 2–3: The lake in Wimbledon
Park at dawn

contents

introduction

For most people today, Wimbledon is synonymous with the famous tennis championships that swell the population of this up-market London suburb in the last week of June and the first week of July every year. The championships had humble origins and the first competitors would not recognize the massively high profile event that takes place today. In 2012 the iconic grass courts will host the tennis event at the Olympics as well as the annual grand slam competition.

Wimbledon has so much more to offer than the tennis however. The wonderful common, four golf courses, Cannizaro House and Park, Wimbledon and Morden Park, greyhound and stock car racing and a football club with a fascinating history.

Wimbledon started life as a small insignificant village in the important manor of Mortlake overseen by the Archbishop of Canterbury. It wasn't really until the Cecil family moved to the manor house in Tudor times, when the church lost control after the dissolution of the monasteries, that it began to figure in the history of England. During Georgian times famous men such as William Wilberforce and Horatio Nelson lived in the area as well as numerous foreign and home secretaries. They were drawn to the place by both its beauty and proximity to London. These wealthy residents brought prestige and employment to the village and it began to grow.

After the railway arrived in the late nineteenth century the area at the bottom of the hill started to be developed and the population exploded. Today Wimbledon is a vibrant, bustling town with a large café culture, theatres and exclusive shops both in the village and in the Centre Court Shopping Centre just down the hill. These days SW19 is a very sought after area in which to live.

Anyone for tennis?

winter

The windmill on Wimbledon
Common covered in snow

'Be nice to your grandmother' was essentially the message of a speech made by Charles, 9th Earl Spencer, when on the 250th anniversary of his family connection with Wimbledon he opened the newly refurbished Wimbledon Museum. That is exactly what his feckless predecessor had done which led to him inheriting her large Wimbledon estate for himself and future generations of his family.

The Spencer family started life as prosperous sheep farmers at the time of the Hundred Years War. By the sixteenth century they owned their estate at Althorp and under the Stuarts, family members entered politics and were rewarded for their services by being given firstly the title of Baron Spencer by James I and later that of the Earl of Sutherland by Charles I. Always influential courtiers, their stock rose even higher when the 33rd Earl of Sutherland married Anne Churchill, daughter of John and Sarah Churchill, Duke and Duchess of Marlborough thus joining two of England's most rich and powerful families. They have continued ever since to provide important colourful characters to our country's history. Sir Winston Churchill and Lady Diana Spencer, Princess of Wales two such illustrious members of the Spencer-Churchill clan.

Sarah Churchill was a shrewd businesswoman and after her husband's death set about increasing the family fortune. She bought over thirty estates one of which was the manor of Wimbledon which included the dilapidated remains of the Manor house, the gardens and the park. She also gained the title 'Lord of the Manor'. There was no love lost between her and her neighbours and she personally wasn't very enamored with the place but did set about building a new house. Her first attempt she hated and decided it was only good enough for servants to live in so she set about building a second close by – she found this slightly more agreeable but was still not completely pleased. The first house was later used by the 1st Earl as a nursery for his many children.

Nicknamed 'Mount Etna' because she was always on the verge of an eruption of temper, she managed to fall out with almost everyone who came into contact with her. This included royalty, prime ministers, architects and most importantly for her grandson John Spencer, all her Churchill relatives. Family feuds were commonplace but she was very fond of her grand daughter Diana, John's sister. Their mother had died young and the formidable old lady had brought them up. It is thought that she refurbished Wimbledon

Manor with Diana in mind. Sadly however, Diana contracted tuberculosis in her twenties and died leaving her grandmother broken hearted and with little appetite to visit Wimbledon again. Her debauched grandson however, used the house regularly to entertain his rowdy friends. He was a gambler and a drunk but also a charmer and his grandmother had a soft spot for him. When in 1744 the old matriarch died she left her personal fortune and Wimbledon to him and his twelve-year-old son. So began the Spencer tenure over the manor of Wimbledon.

John's unhealthy lifestyle quickly caught up with him however, and he died aged thirty-eight only two years after his eighty-five-year-old grandmother, having never enjoyed his inheritance. His son, still a minor, inherited the estate. Initially it was overseen by trustees but on coming of age the young John Spencer took an active part in the estate affairs. Shortly after he took control of the manor he employed the famous landscape gardener Lancelot 'Capability' Brown to make improvements to the park area. In six years it was transformed into a place 'as beautiful as anything near London'. Brown drained a swampy area and linked two old fishponds making a Serpentine Lake – his trademark feature, that still remains today, enjoyed by so many. He also replaced the old straight drive to the house with a new winding route. The gatehouse lodge keeper in the early 1800s was Robert Tibbet and he lends his name to the roundabout at the top of Putney Hill – Tibbet's Corner.

George, the 2nd Earl was born in Wimbledon and baptized at St Mary's Church. He was brought up in the nursery house, the house that his great, great grandmother had built and hated. As a schoolboy he believed Wimbledon to be 'the prettiest place in the world'. When he grew up he spent a lot of time there despite his wife's objections – she didn't love the place quite as much as her husband! Tragedy hit in March 1785 when the house caught fire and was burnt to a cinder. The earl had to decide whether to re-build or not. Given his wife's antipathy to the place and his growing debts he decided instead to re-furbish the nursery. It was at this time that a well was dug and constructed. Hundreds of feet deep it was a major undertaking and the well house remains today – an unusual and unique residential property on Arthur Road.

George Spencer's day job was First Lord of the Admiralty, an important position at the time because England was at

Frozen lake

war with Napoleonic France. His most famous Admiral – Lord Nelson lived just down the road in Merton Place. Given this fact it was strange that the two rarely met socially – a major snub for Nelson. Reading Spencer's wife Lavinia's letters explains why. Originally she said of Nelson 'how perfectly he fulfills my notion of a Christian hero'. He then left his wife and took up with Lady Hamilton and suddenly he became 'the little man between that old fool and his wife' whose 'disgusting bragging and vanity makes me want to vomit'. No wonder they never had them round to dinner!

It was during George's tenure as Lord of the Manor that the common began to be a problem. For years it had been the right of commoners to graze their cattle and take gravel and firewood for their own use but by the turn of the nineteenth century 'evil-disposed outsiders' had moved in and gypsy encampments had led to depravity and lawlessness on the common. The Earl attempted to enclose it as private property but wealthy local residents objected and he dropped his plans. As he got older his extravagant lifestyle meant that he lived well beyond his rather large means and he fell more and more heavily into debt. One helpful remedy to ease his financial situation was to rent out Wimbledon Park House to the Duke of Somerset.

The 3rd Earl not only inherited his father's title and properties but also his debt. To raise immediate cash he sold Wimbledon Park House and its land to property developer John Augustus Beaumont but remained Lord of the Manor. Beaumont saw the potential in the land as the arrival of the railways in southwest London would increase the demand for suburban housing. To make more money the Earl's steward had started excising large quantities of gravel from the common to sell for profit. The Wimbledon Vestry objected and the practice stopped but the gravel pits remain today. The 3rd Earl died after only ten years in charge of the family. His brother Frederick became the 4th Earl but he only lasted another twelve years before popping off and leaving his son John in charge as the 5th Earl.

Although he had no real contact with Wimbledon and had never lived there he was instrumental in setting up the National Rifle Association's link with Wimbledon Common. A keen marksman he encouraged 'his common's' use as a rifle range. Napoleon III was an increasing threat and Englishmen were being encouraged to establish Volunteer Forces to be mobilized against the French if necessary. Rifle shooting practice was encouraged and competitions provided lucrative prize money enticements to entrants. In 1866 prize money

at the Wimbledon event was £8,884 a sizable amount at the time.

Queen Victoria shot the inaugural bullet to open the first meeting in 1860. These meetings carried on until 1889. The population of Wimbledon had been steadily increasing and it was decided that the public wandering freely about the common caused too great a problem and it was only matter of time before a stray bullet hit some innocent person. The National Rifle Association and its meetings were moved to Bisley where they remain today.

In 1864 the 5th Earl, like his predecessor attempted to enclose the common. Yet again his efforts were thwarted by locals who feared the common once 'tamed' might like the park be sold off for housing development. A Wimbledon and Putney Commons Committee was formed to fight the plan. They were supported by the Commons Preservation Society which had already helped Blackheath and Hampstead Heath escape enclosure. In 1871 the Earl admitted defeat and gave up his rights over the common to a body of elected conservators. He was in return paid £1,200 a year – this arrangement lasted until 1968.

This was the end of the Spencers' involvement in Wimbledon. They had left their mark however. Spencer Road, the Well House, the gravel pits on the common and the Capability Brown designed lake in Wimbledon Park all legacies of their stay as Lords of the Manor.

St Mary's Church

Rushmere Pond in the snow

Homeward bound after
a hack in the snow
RIGHT: Tobogganing fun

the wombles

Underground, overground, wombling free,
The Wombles of Wimbledon Common are we.
Making good use of the things we have found
Things that the everyday folks leave behind.

The words of the chorus to the song *The Wombling Song* hint at the green message that was at the heart of The Wombles' mission. Their motto 'to make good use of bad rubbish' was launched in 1968, years ahead of its time and long before recycling was an everyday occurrence.

The stories about The Wombles were written by Elizabeth Beresford. After a family Christmas with elderly relatives Elizabeth took her two young children to Wimbledon Common to let off steam. After running about excitedly, her daughter returned to her exclaiming 'Isn't it fun on Wombledon Common'. Inspired by an idea the already prolific writer Elizabeth went home and started to pen stories about The Wombles of Wimbledon Common. All of The Wombles were based on family members with the elderly patriarch Great Uncle Bulgaria being a thinly disguised version of her father-in-law and the young rather lazy, greedy Orinoco based somewhat unflatteringly on her own teenage son.

The stories were at first read on the children's television story time programme *Jackanory*. They went down so well that The Wombles were given their own programme with the furry characters' words being narrated by Bernard Cribbins. This led to The Wombles releasing records, being portrayed on stage and in a feature film *Wombling Free* in 1977. Their avid cleaning up led them to be the symbol of the 'Keep Britain Tidy' advertising campaign of the 1970s. The message seemed to work with children setting up 'Womble cleaning-up groups' on Wimbledon Common and elsewhere. Anecdotal evidence also suggests it may have added to litter with younger children dropping rubbish intentionally with the hope of Wombles coming out of hiding to clear it up!

Elizabeth Beresford was born into a literary family with her father being the author JD Beresford. Growing up she was always in the company of the greats of the literary world such as DH Lawrence, HG Wells and Rudyard Kipling with Walter de la Mare her godfather. As a young woman she ghost wrote speeches for Conservative MPs and went on to work for the BBC on the *Today* programme and *Woman's Hour*. She started writing children's books in the 1960s.

The heyday of The Wombles' popularity was the 1970s but in November 2010 publishers Bloomsbury reissued The Womble books re-launching the series during the Wimbledon Book Festival at an event on Wimbledon Common. Although in ill health, Elizabeth Beresford was said to be overjoyed at her Wombles' reemergence. She died on Christmas Eve 2010 with the knowledge that her furry creations lived on.

LEFT: Uncle Bulgaria near Rushmere Pond at the re-launch of The Wombles books
RIGHT: Uncle Bulgaria surveying the common

Cannizaro Park
RIGHT: Mandarine ducks
on the frozen pond

A dormant tennis venue

Fighting the blizzard on
the common

LEFT: A chilly Diana
RIGHT: A cold winter's morning
on the common

population explosion

The population of Wimbledon swelled from 2,693 recorded in the 1851 census to 41,652 just fifty years later, a sixteen fold increase. The reason for this seismic increase was the industrial revolution and the building of the railways. Like so many small towns and villages on the perimeter of London the arrival of the railways changed Wimbledon forever.

The fire-breathing machine which frightened yet excited so many Victorians had a profound effect on social, economic and political life in the whole of Britain. Travel, once a preserve of the rich became accessible for the middle and working classes. People started taking day trips and short holidays to the seaside. Commuting to work began. British time became standardized because the trains had to set a timetable across the whole country. Many sports which were run locally before, became nationally regulated and national football, rugby and cricket competitions began. National newspapers could be delivered to the whole country by train so knowledge of the state of current affairs and events became more widespread. The population as a whole became politically more aware and empowered as a result. Regional goods such as fresh fish and vegetables were delivered quickly to areas that had previously been out of reach. The railway industry with its locomotives, tracks, and accessories became one of Britain's best exports and a huge employer, all helping the country's economy to grow enormously. It truly was a revolution.

The sleepy, wealthy Georgian village at the top of the hill around the common was transformed into a bustling, overcrowded Victorian town that grew up at the bottom of the hill around the railway tracks and stations. The evolution of Wimbledon began in 1838 when the first railway arrived. It came from Nine Elms near Vauxhall and went to Woking via Surbiton. Over the next few years however, extra tracks were opened to West Croydon, Epsom, Tooting and Kingston, and Wimbledon became an important railway junction. Middle class commuters moved into large houses between the common and the station and much cheaper terraced housing was erected on the farm land to the south to provide accommodation for the working classes who were drawn to the area in search of work on the railways, in construction and in domestic service. This area was often overcrowded and insanitary and regular outbreaks of typhoid, diphtheria and scarlet fever meant that the death rate of those living south of the railway was twice as high as those at the top of the hill. The rapid population growth began to plateau off by the turn of the century but by then the area had changed completely never to return to its former self.

The main national railway is not the only form of transport that Wimbledon had been exposed to. The Wandle Valley thirty-five years before had seen the opening of Britain's first public railway – The Surrey Iron Railway, the first railway company to be sanctioned by Parliament. Not strictly a railway with trains, it was in fact an iron track along which a horse pulled carts laden with goods at the grand speed of three miles an hour. Although it didn't last very long it was historically significant because it initiated the legal framework on which the national rail network was later based.

Some years later a similar horse drawn railway carriage was to be found in use on Wimbledon Common transporting people from the pond in Wimbledon Village to the Windmill during the National Rifle Shooting Association's annual competitions. It was first installed in 1864 and was dismantled at the end of each annual competition only to resurface again the following year. It proved very popular and profitable and in 1877 the horse was replaced by a steam engine. Original plans for a major railway line from Putney had tracks crossing the common but luckily for today's residents these plans were shelved and the track diverted elsewhere. Today's common, a haven of tranquility in a busy London suburb, would have been a very different place with a railway track through the middle of it.

LEFT: The busy mainline
connecting Wimbledon to Waterloo
RIGHT: The Croydon tram line

Wimbledon Common at dusk

Wimbledon Park
RIGHT: Robin Redbreast puffed
up against the winter chill

Winter scenes from the common

No.1 Court catches some early sunlight
on a beautiful winter's morning

spring

Bluebells on the common

Wimbledon Park early on a spring morning

Sunrise over the park

mills of merton

'The hardest working river in the world for its size' is how the River Wandle has been described. Only nine miles long, at one stage up to ninety watermills were drawing power from the river. Springs in the North Downs feed into the short river which meanders its way through the borough of Merton past South Wimbledon, Wimbledon, Wimbledon Park, Southfields, and Earlsfield to enter the Thames at Wandsworth. It was always useless for navigation because of its steep descent and fast flowing water but this made it ideal for efficiently supplying waterpower to mills. Predominantly the mills ground corn to supply the capital with flour but there were also mills working copper, iron, leather, paper, snuff and gunpowder as well as the important textile printing industry. It was a hugely important area to the London economy.

Some of the mills still exist today although they are no longer in use. One such at Morden Hall was a renowned snuff mill. There was also a snuff mill at Ravensbury where the proprietor John Rutter produced 'Mitcham Shag' a notable snuff. Ravensbury Mill was the last working mill on the river closing in the 1960s. The Morden Park snuff mill produced this popular drug from the mid 1750s until the 1920s.

Sir John Hawkins introduced tobacco to England, possibly as early as 1565. The popularity of 'tobacco drinking' as it was known or smoking as we now know it gradually increased in popularity but it was made truly fashionable by Sir Walter Raleigh in the Elizabethan Court. Early Englishmen smoked tobacco following the North American Indian habit. South American Indians however preferred to take their tobacco in powder form up their nose. Spanish Conquistadores copied the snuff habit and it was them who brought snuff back to Europe. The taking of snuff spread across France to England, its heyday being in the Regency Period when George IV had an entire room at Windsor Castle dedicated to the powder. A man would be judged by his 'blend' and snuff boxes were important accessories to the dandified clothing of the day.

Not everyone was so enamored with the stuff though. In 1624 Pope Urban VII threatened to excommunicate anyone taking snuff in church and Tsar Michael of Russia went even further. He chopped snuff takers' noses off for their first offense and executed them for their second!

Eventually though the habit declined in popularity and the addiction to tobacco was replaced by another form of the leaf. The cigarette, introduced into Britain after the Crimean War, had become the drug of choice of the country by the end of World War I. The end was nigh for the snuff mills of the Wandle.

Snuff production was an evil process. Workers equipped with water soaked sponge respirators ground the dried tobacco in intolerable conditions. When the weather was hot production often had to stop as the working environment became too dangerous. The National Trust now owns the Morden Park snuff mill.

The Wandle Trail now follows the River Wandle on the whole of its journey from source to Thames and is a credit to the hard work of local people who have restored the river and its towpath into a pleasant walk or cycle from a grim, polluted, rubbish strewn river classified as a sewer in the not too dim and distant past into the clean, clear, free, fast flowing waterway it is today.

Daffodils in Morden Hall Park and watermills on the Wandle

Sunshine and showers, typical
April weather at Rushmere Pond

the tudors

Wimbledon's relative insignificance in history began to change in Tudor times. Henry VIII's disagreement with the Pope led to the formation of the Church of England and the breaking away from the dominance of Rome. Many Catholic churches and monasteries were destroyed and tension between Catholics and Protestants has remained to this day in many parts of the world.

The manor of Mortlake of which Wimbledon was a part had always been under the jurisdiction of the Archbishop of Canterbury. Thomas Cranmer was the incumbent Archbishop at the time of these religious upheavals and he prudently decided to give the manor to the King. Although officially owned by the crown the residing monarch never visited or paid much attention to the manor just leasing parts of it to various influential people.

One such person was Sir William Cecil, who leased the rectory for his family to live in. He was the chief advisor to Queen Elizabeth I for most of her reign and therefore an incredibly powerful man. His family grew up in Wimbledon and his oldest son Thomas rather competitively went on to build a huge Tudor manor house near his father's home. By all accounts it was magnificent – good enough in fact to attract several visits from Queen Elizabeth herself so putting Wimbledon on the map. Royal visits were hugely important to a local economy. The entourage was usually enormous so many services were necessary to cater for them. Rich people were drawn to the fashionable area and poor people followed in their wake looking for employment. Sir Thomas was responsible for improving the roads in the area making the commute to London easier.

One such grandee was Robert Bell who built a mansion on the High Street now known as Eagle House. It is considered to be one of the finest examples of a Jacobean house still surviving in London. Robert Bell made his name and fortune as one of the co-founders of the East India Company. This company traded mainly in cotton, silk, tea, pepper and opium. Its importance grew in the Indian sub-continent to the extent that it ruled large areas of the country. It exercised military and political power and was intricately linked to the British Empire's control of India which was only relinquished just after the World War II.

Sir Thomas Cecil's grand house was later bought by Charles I for his Queen, Henrietta Maria. She lived there first as his wife and then his widow after his execution and later after the restoration as the Dowager Queen, mother of Charles II. In 1661 it was sold to the Earl of Bristol.

By now the movers and the shakers of the time were beginning to reside in Wimbledon as they have been doing ever since. For this reason Sir Thomas Cecil is often referred to as 'the maker of Wimbledon'.

Eagle House

Bluebells in the woods on the common

Crocuses in Cannizaro Park

FC to AFC

The history of football in Wimbledon is both interesting and acrimonious. The team of the 1980s was famously known as 'the crazy gang', with notorious footballer turned actor Vinnie Jones their most (in)famous player. Theirs was a fairy tale story of David vs. Goliath when the unfashionable Wimbledon beat the mighty Liverpool to lift the FA cup in 1988.

There has been a football team in Wimbledon since the Wimbledon Old Central Football Club was formed in 1889. The team got its name from the Old Central School on Wimbledon Common where its players had been pupils. Matches took place on the common and players used to celebrate victories and losses at the Fox and Grapes pub, the team head quarters. In 1905 the 'Old Central' was dropped from the name and in 1912 Wimbledon FC moved to Plough Lane. The team stayed there for over seventy years until the fallout from the Hillsborough disaster meant that the Plough Lane Stadium was not considered fit for purpose and in 1990 Wimbledon FC temporarily moved in with Crystal Palace at Selhurst Park. This temporary arrangement lasted for twelve years with the club in discussions with Merton Council over either the redevelopment of the Plough Lane site or the Wimbledon Stadium. During this time the fortunes of the team declined, they were relegated and gate revenues dropped. In 2001 the club announced it was relocating to the town of Milton Keynes. This decision outraged the fans who boycotted games and set up the rival AFC Wimbledon team. With attendances at Selhurst Park plummeting money dried up and the club went into administration in 2003. In 2004 Wimbledon FC were rebranded The Milton Keynes Dons or 'MK Dons'. AFC Wimbledon set up home at the Kingsmeadow ground in Kingston from where they continue to look for a permanent ground back in Wimbledon.

Wimbledon FC had languished in the amateur league for many years slowly making progress up the divisions before being promoted and elected to the professional league in 1977. The next ten years saw their meteoric rise through the professional leagues, ending up in the old first division and later the premier league for fourteen glorious years between 1986 and 2000. They even managed a foray in Europe competing in the Intertoto Cup.

AFC Wimbledon is hoping to emulate the old Wimbledon team. In the ten years since their formation they have been promoted repeatedly, at one stage going seventy-eight games without loss, an all time record in English senior football. In the summer of 2011 they won an exciting penalty shoot out in the play off final of the non-leagues' top division, the National Conference which took them out of the non-league once again and into division two of the N-Power League. Each week the team is led out onto the pitch by their mascot Haydon the Womble whilst around three thousand fans cheer on. To celebrate this achievement the club was given the honour of opening the Wimbledon Fair an event held annually in June on Wimbledon Common.

In 2011 in the FA Cup there was a possibility of MK Dons playing AFC Wimbledon. This possible fixture caused serious worries within the football community because of the potential for trouble, such is the strength of feeling amongst the AFC fans. Even after all these years, memories of the perceived treachery cause feelings to run incredibly high in this most tribal of games.

Match day and the mascot Haydon The Womble with two young fans

Spring is here, gorse in flower and
new growth on the common

textile tributory

Liberty prints and William Morris prints and wallpapers are designs famous the world over. Dating back to the late nineteenth and early twentieth century, they have stood the test of time and are as popular today as they were then. They were originally manufactured in the Wandle Valley near South Wimbledon. The River Wandle, a fast flowing chalk stream had been associated with the textile industry for centuries.

Cotton was produced in the Indian sub-continent. Medieval Europeans didn't know how cotton was made and there was what now seems a preposterous idea that it was obtained from trees that grew lambs. In 1350 it was written 'there grew in India a wonderful tree which bore tiny lambs on the end of its branches. These branches so pliable that they bent down to allow the lambs to feed when they are hungrie'.

The manufacture of cotton continued to remain a secret for many years but the finished printed cotton or 'chintz' was imported into England by the East India Company and by the end of the seventeenth century had became hugely popular. The powerful wool trade lobbied parliament to act against this product that was harming the local industries by providing cheap, attractive, popular alternatives to wool clothing. Laws were passed banning the import of printed cotton. To get round this early form of protectionism the traders instead imported the rough form of the textile which arrived as a drab brown material known as calico. This then had to be bleached and printed to make it a saleable product. The Dutch had perfected the bleaching techniques and most calico was sent there initially before returning to England for printing. Some Dutch bleachers or 'whitesters' as they were appropriately known, relocated to the Wandle Valley in the 1660s and started a calico bleaching and silk manufacturing business on the banks of the river. Bunces Meadow was a large bleaching field situated on the site between Deen City Farm and the tram line on the borders of Morden Hall Park. Row upon row of water filled ditches were covered with lengths of calico which after some chemical processes were left outside all summer to bleach in the sun.

As well as the arrival of Dutch bleachers the area also became home to the first 'refugees'. They were the French Protestant Huguenots who took 'refuge' in England, escaping from religious persecution and the death penalty in France under the orders of the Catholic King Louis XIV. They arrived in droves in England – an estimated two hundred thousand fled. They were not welcomed with open arms with the English fearing for their jobs – sound familiar? Many Huguenots worked in the textile industry in their native France and brought their skills in dying, printing, felt and hat making with them to England. A number established themselves in the calico printing trade and set up shop in the Wandle Valley. The first calico print works was established in 1724, it thrived and over the next two hundred years hundreds of local people were employed in the textile industry.

William Morris and Arthur Liberty were both working from Merton Abbey in the latter part of the nineteenth century. Liberty began his career at sixteen working for a relative who was a lace maker. He was hugely impressed and influenced by Japanese design and when he began managing Farmers and Rogers Great Shawl Emporium he was instrumental in the store's specialization in the sale of oriental goods. He was a brilliant businessman, predicting important trends, and in his later career driving those trends. He had many artist friends and was closely associated with the Pre-Raphaelite group, the Arts and Craft Movement and Art Nouveau which is still

referred to in Italy as 'Style Liberty'. He opened a shop in Regents Street known originally as 'East India House' which later became 'Libertys'. It remains one of the landmarks of the London shopping scene today. One of its trademarks then and now was its beautiful fabrics. From 1874 many of these were made at the print works at Merton Abbey by Edmund Littler especially for Liberty. In 1904 Liberty bought his business, and goods continued to be produced there for the store up until 1972.

William Morris was part of the same 'set' and he knew Liberty well. He is considered the single most influential designer of his time and remains today one of the best known of all British designers. He founded a design business with Pre-Raphaelite artists Edward Burne-Jones and Dante Gabriel Rossetti (an old boy of King's College School, Wimbledon). His company was responsible for designing and printing fabric, tapestry, wallpaper, stained glass, tiles and furniture. He later started a new company called Morris

and Co. and moved it into premises at Merton Abbey. He was a workaholic, and as well as his designing he was renowned as a writer, poet, environmentalist, political thinker and philosopher. He is closely linked with the emergence of Socialism. He died aged sixty-five it is said 'of the disease of hard work' a great mind and a great man. His workshops at Merton Abbey continued producing goods until 1940 when Libertys took over the site.

Today, in amongst the industrial estate on the site of the old priory, Merton Abbey Mill remains – the buildings much as they were over a hundred years ago. It is still described as a craft village with a craft market taking place every weekend and antique markets in the week. The restored water wheel at the mill still turns in the summer and the William Morris pub situated on the river is a haven of tranquility in amongst the hubbub of a busy London district. This area with its rich history has been lovingly restored of late and is a credit to the local people responsible.

The small wetland area in Morden Hall Park

Spring in Cannizaro Park

the georgians

The era of Hanoverian rule in England began in 1714 with the arrival of George I. He spoke no English and was totally disinterested in running the country. This marked the beginning of the power of the prime minister and the cabinet system of running the government that we know today. Three more Georges followed him and their reigns saw major upheavals in world politics. It was during George III's reign that most events occurred. He at least could speak English but unfortunately the poor man suffered from regular bouts of insanity during which he was unable to run the country so again his government became hugely influential in decision-making.

His reign started well with the winning of the Seven Years War, the first major global military conflict involving the major European powers, all vying for control over the various colonies in other continents. It ended with Britain controlling both India and America. It was a short-lived victory however, within a few years everything had changed.

The Americans rebelled and the American War of Independence followed which ended in a British defeat and the formation of the United States of America. Following the American revolutionary success the French tried their luck and succeeded in overthrowing their monarchy, which saw the creation of the first French Republic. This led to a long period of intermittent war in Europe with various alliances fighting the French and the rise of Napoleon to Emperor.

In the middle of this the Irish rebelled and had to be dealt with. With many of the major political players of the time living in and around the area, Wimbledon saw its fair share of involvement in the political decisions of this tumultuous time.

Earl Spencer, First Lord of the Admiralty and later Home Secretary, lived at Wimbledon Park. Henry Dundas, 1st Viscount Melville, Home Secretary and First Lord of the Admiralty lived at Cannizaro House. William Grenville, Pitt's cousin, Foreign Secretary and later Prime Minister lived at Eagle House. Wiliam Wilberforce MP and the man responsible for the abolition of slavery lived at Lauriston House, and Pitt the Younger the Prime Minister for most of George III's reign was friends with them all and although he never lived in Wimbledon visited regularly. Down the road at Merton Place lived Admiral Nelson when he was in the country. These were the men who were shaping history at the time and they all lived within a stone's throw of each other in Wimbledon Village.

FAR LEFT: A reminder of an old Wimbledon resident
LEFT: The Well built by Earl Spencer in 1763 was converted into a residence in 1975
RIGHT: Crocuses in front of the aviary in Cannizaro Park

Cricket and sailing, just two of the
activities possible in Wimbledon Park

summer

One of several panels inset into the new
walls surrounding the All England Lawn
Tennis Club

Icons of a summer in SW19

anyone for jeu de paume?

The All England Croquet Club situated in Worple Road Wimbledon, so legend has it, were a bit short of money and needed a new roller to keep their grass in good condition. They decided to hold a tennis tournament to raise some money and so in 1877 the inaugural Wimbledon tennis tournament was held. The competitors had to put up with the sound of gun fire from the National Rifle Association's competition on Wimbledon Common which at the time was a much more popular event. The tennis tournament was won by Spencer Gore who, after his victory said of the sport that 'it is boring and will never catch on'. He might have been good at tennis but was dreadful at predicting the future! The All England Croquet Club became the All England Lawn Tennis and Croquet Club and has been responsible for the annual tournament ever since even though the croquet in its name is an all but forgotten memory.

In the 1880s the dynamic Renshaw brothers started the serve-volley craze that made the game very exciting to watch and the tournament became ever more popular. Ladies were allowed to play from 1884, and in 1912 the French player Suzanne Lenglen shocked audiences by playing in an outfit that revealed her calves and did not include a corset. She became a style icon with her bobbed haircut being widely copied.

The tournament quickly outgrew its Worple Road ground and in 1922 moved to its present location on Church Road where it was opened by King George V. This move was considered a real financial risk at the time but over the years it

has proved to be a great investment. By 1926 the game was proving so popular that a professional circuit was started. However, Wimbledon remained open only to amateurs. By 1967 the situation had become untenable, with all good players turning professional the importance of the Wimbledon champions title was diminshed. It was decided to make the tournament 'open' heralding a new era in tennis.

The new millennium was a wonderful time in men's tennis with the emergence of two of the greatest competitors ever to have played the game. In the 2008 men's final, Roger Federer, rated the greatest grass court player of all time, played Raphael Nadal, rated the greatest clay court player of all time. It is widely considered the most exciting and best quality tennis final ever played with Nadal eventually winning 9–7 in the fifth set as darkness fell. The match had lasted 4 hours 48 minutes, the longest time taken to complete the final in the history of the tournament. Nadal had become the man who ended Federer's grass court winning streak of sixty-five consecutive matches and the first to win back-to-back French Open and Wimbledon tournaments since the great Bjorn Borg in 1980.

However, Federer refused to be thrown off his stride and returned the following year having just won in France. Although he proved that the difficult task of winning on clay and then grass as well was not beyond him, his victory was far from straightforward. He met American Andy Roddick in the final. After another long, hard fought five setter, the longest final in history in terms of games played, Federer eventually won the

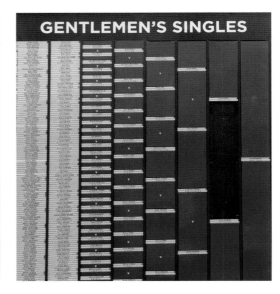

Members of the All England Tennis and Croquet Club, taking part in the less famous more sedate game still played at the club

fifth set 16−14, the longest last set in history − by this time the records were tumbling. This win meant that Federer had won fifteen grand slams, more than any other player in the history of the game making him arguably the greatest men's tennis player of all time.

For two weeks in June and July every year, thousands of people visit Wimbledon swelling the population of the town. The event is famous throughout the world. It is not only the tennis that attracts. Wimbledon fortnight is on the social calendar and nothing could be more pleasant than sipping a glass of (very) expensive champagne whilst tucking into a bowl of (very) expensive strawberries and cream having just watched a fantastic tennis match on the beautifully prepared green, green grass of Wimbledon. It is one of those British icons like the Houses of Parliament or red buses and long may it continue.

The lovely rose garden in
Wimbledon Park

A large family of swans on Queensmere Lake

sw19 tennis postcode

'It must be a comedy if a British player is winning Wimbledon' so said Serena Williams about the 2004 film *Wimbledon* in which a British journeyman pro ranked 119 in the world is given a wild card to the tournament, falls in love with a beautiful American and ends up winning the title. The wild card entrant's winning tale is based on Goran Ivanisevic's remarkable journey in 2001 from down and out, in tennis terms, to Wimbledon Champion beating along the way, with a bit of help from our unpredictable weather, the perennial semi-finalist, our own Tim Henman. The romance drew its story line from the handsome British player John Lloyd who married the pretty American champion Chris Evert in 1979. The British player winning is however, complete fiction so far...

Originally when the tournament began in 1877 we produced many homegrown champions but then again we did have a head start on the rest of the world by inventing lawn tennis. Mirroring what has happened in football and cricket, other games we invented, as soon as the other countries started playing and transport was good enough for them to get to competitions, they began to beat us! This has been a continuing trend now for too long. Since Fred Perry won three years running in 1934, 1935 and 1936 no British man

has won Wimbledon. Bunny Austin, Mike Sangster, Roger Taylor, Tim Henman and Andy Murray have all reached the semi-finals but as yet no one has progressed any further in the last seventy years or so. Poor old Tim Henman made it to the semis four times. Unlike in cricket however, when a pitch is prepared with the home team in mind, just when we had one of the best serve-volleyers in the game, the Wimbledon committee decided to slow the game down. In their wisdom they made the grass and the balls slower, all playing into the hands of the accurate base liners who sat in wait for 'our Tim', passing him with ease as he ran gallantly to the net. He never had a chance with even the authorities against him! A bit of an own goal to mix sporting terms.

The women have faired slightly better, Virginia Wade won the ladies' singles title, playing in front of the Queen (a reluctant fan apparently) in the centenary year of 1977 a mere thirty years ago. Sue Barker who now commentates for the BBC during Wimbledon was also a semi-finalist that year. She also has the dubious honour of having dated Sir Cliff Richards – another Wimbledon favourite who, in 1996 famously entertained Centre Court during one of the frequent showers so often endured by the Wimbledon crowd. Joined by ex-players Virginia Wade, Pam Shriver and Martina

The statue of Fred Perry, the last British Wimbledon winner and Roger Federer's shoes advertising the fact that he has won the singles title six times

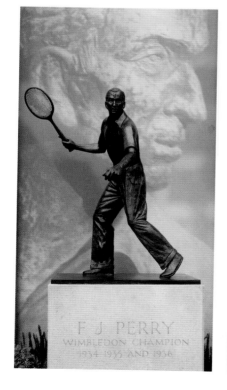

Navratilova amongst others he got the whole crowd singing *Summer Holiday* whilst the rain fell down. It is a relief to some that with the advances in technology the retractable roof over Centre Court means that this will never be repeated again.

Henman may not have won Wimbledon but his memory does live on in the form of a hill. During his epic struggle with Ivanisevic during the 2001 semi-final the aforementioned Sue Barker, whilst commentating, referred to the slope behind the Centre Court, where adoring crowds had accumulated to watch the match on the big screen, as Henman Hill. The name stuck and it is still referred to as such today. Every year commentators try to change it depending on who is playing. It has been Rudsedski Ridge and Murray Mound but neither of those names have stuck and true fans still use the original name. Henman also has another far more surprising Wimbledon claim to fame – he is the only player ever to have been disqualified at Wimbledon surpassing even

John McEnroe and Jeff Tarangos' bad behaviour for which they were only fined. In a fit of pique whilst playing a doubles match early in his career he struck a ball in anger. It hit a poor ball girl smack in the forehead and felled her to the ground and Henman was summarily dismissed. A blemish in his otherwise spotless career and he did send her some flowers as an apology.

Given our hapless attempts to win back the Wimbledon crown there is another solution. Rather than keep trying to produce British winners it might be easier to just invent a new game. We seem rather good at that and at least it would guarantee a winner for a few years until the rest of the world caught up!

The tennis isn't always riveting.
A typical English summer –
umbrellas always come in handy
RIGHT BELOW: Covers on

ABOVE: A poppy in
Wimbledon Park
BELOW: A moorhen floats
about in the waterlillies on
Queensmere Pond

Diana with a flower
in her hair

watch the birdie

There are four golf courses in close proximity to the All England Tennis Club, the official name for where Wimbledon tennis tournament is played. These are the London Scottish, Wimbledon Common and Royal Wimbledon clubs and are all located on or around the common and Wimbledon Park.

Queen Victoria visited Scotland regularly during her reign and many of her subjects followed her north of the border for their holidays. There they were introduced to the game of 'gouf'. As a result of this exposure the game become increasingly popular in England. It had been played informally on the common for many years when in 1864 members of the London Scottish Rifle Volunteers who were billeted nearby formed the London Scottish Golf Club. Initially the course only had seven holes but in 1871 an eighteen-hole course was set out before the newly formed Commons Conservators could object. It was one of only three official golf clubs in the country at the time, the others being Blackheath and Westward-Ho in Devon. By 1880 the civilian members of the club outnumbered the military members 4-1. Their subscriptions however, were eight times those of their fellow military members and to add insult to injury they had no voting rights. This naturally caused immense resentment and in 1881 the club split in two. The London Scottish Club head quarters remained by the windmill near Mrs Doggett's Cottage and the newly formed Wimbledon Golf Club moved to the other side of the common. A year after the move the club was bestowed with the title 'Royal' by the Queen whose son, the future Edward VII, Prince of Wales was a member. The Earl of Wemyss, the club captain from1881-1894, resigned in disgust when the Common Conservators passed a by-law insisting all players 'wear a red coat or other red garment' when playing on the common in the interests of safety, a tradition that remains today. This may or may not be related to the club moving premises again in 1907. They moved to the area known as 'Caesars Camp' looking over the valley towards Kingston making it a much hillier course than the common. The Wimbledon Town Golf Club remained on the old site sharing the course with the London Scottish but teeing off at the first at opposite ends next to their respective clubhouses.

Wimbledon Park was rescued from development by the Wimbledon Corporation who bought the park to retain it for recreational purposes. Many locals objected, saying it was a waste of public money but luckily for today's residents they lost and it remained a park. The Wimbledon Park Sports club was created promoting cricket, curling, fishing, shooting and golf. The cricket, tennis and golf clubs remain today. The golf club opened in 1898 and the course follows the bend of the lake laid out by 'Capability' Brown over a hundred years before. Each year part of the course is closed to provide parking for the Wimbledon tennis tournament across the road.

FAR LEFT: Golf in Wimbledon Park
NEAR LEFT: Golf on the Common
RIGHT: Golf at Royal Wimbledon

All the fun of the fair. An annual event on the common

Beautiful wildflowers on the common

bangers, bikes and greyhounds

A few miles down the road from the sedate stadium known as Centre Court is the other Wimbledon Stadium. Located on Plough Lane it hosts greyhound racing three nights a week and in the winter the Demolition Derby, where old cars battle it out to be the last one running. Up until 2005 Speedway was also held here. The biking Wimbledon Dons Speedway team raced at the stadium for nearly eighty years.

The stadium was built specifically for greyhound racing. Greyhounds have huge hearts and numerous fast twitch muscles in their lithe bodies making them the fastest dogs on earth, capable of reaching speeds of forty-five miles an hour. Similar dogs date back to Egyptian times when they were revered and where mummified and buried alongside the ancient kings. They are the only dogs mentioned in the bible and have always had a special place alongside man. They are classified as sight hounds – catching their prey by having good eyesight, being agile and very quick over a short distance.

In 1014 King Canute, the Danish king, introduced Forest Law into England. This forbade amongst other things the use of dogs for hunting by anyone other than the aristocracy. Punishments were harsh (death if you killed a stag) but that didn't stop the peasants from keeping hunting dogs to provide valuable food for their families. Whilst aristocrats favoured white, pure looking dogs, the peasants bred brindle dogs that blended into the forest vegetation. Such dogs were supposed to have three toes cut off or their hamstrings severed so they could not hunt. Forest Law remained in place for 700 years and although it had been largely ignored for much of that time it wasn't until the 1831 Game Act that coursing became legal. It was finally made illegal again in 2005.

Hare coursing had been practiced for hundreds of years with Queen Elizabeth I being particularly fond of the sport. The Duke of Norfolk drew up the English hare coursing rules during Elizabeth I's reign. Two hounds raced, being awarded points for 'speed, go-bye, turn, wrench, kill and trip'. The first club was opened in Swatham in Norfolk in 1776. It gradually grew in popularity with gambling going on at the meets. The only problem was that there was a limited number of people that could congregate on a field or common. This led to two entrepreneurs in America inventing the artificial lure and building an oval track to race it around so more people could watch and more gambling could go on. After numerous false starts and mishaps with the technology they eventually manufactured a working model and modern greyhound racing had begun.

In 1924, back in the UK, on nearby Morden Common Henry Amos and some of his friends were campaigning against rabbit coursing as a cruel sport. They went on to establish the League Against Cruel Sports. This campaign coincided with the rights to use the artificial lure being bought by American businessman Charles Munn who built the first greyhound stadium in England at Belle Vue, Manchester and established the Greyhound Racing Association. On 24 July 1926, 1,700 people watched the first greyhound race in the UK. Due to the success of this venture other stadiums were quickly erected all over the country, Wimbledon being one of them. Racing in Wimbledon had begun and this was the beginning of the end for the previously popular sport of coursing.

At about this time, a sport that had begun in New South Wales, Australia called Speedway was also becoming popular in the UK. Four men on motorbikes with no brakes and one gear, race and slide their way around a dirt track in search of victory. The two sports were a perfect partnership both utilizing the same track so maximizing the earning potential of the stadium. The Wimbledon Dons completed their first race in 1928 and remained a fixture at the stadium until a few years ago. Stock car racing joined the fun in the 1960s and is still a popular attraction weekly through the winter months.

Greyhound and stock car racing at the stadium on Plough Lane

autumn

An autumn morning on the common

nelson and lady hamilton

Lord Horatio Nelson and Lady Emma Hamilton, two of the areas most famous past residents, lived locally at Merton Place at the beginning of the nineteenth century. The house subsequently fell into disrepair and was unfortunately demolished but the story of their time there lives on – a fascinating tale of scandal and glamour. Their lives intrigued and outraged both the local and wider population with their peculiar living arrangements, which even today would be considered out of the ordinary.

Their first significant meeting was in Naples. Famous beauty meets famous hero. Both vain, they were instantly attracted to each other and fell in love with each other and the notoriety the other brought. They could possibly be considered the first celebrity couple, with the press of the day clamouring for any tit-bits of gossip including trivia such as what they ate for dinner.

Theirs is an unusual story. Amy Lyon, as Emma was christened, was a blacksmith's daughter brought up by her grandmother in Wales. She entered service at a young age and by her sixteenth year she was living with Mrs Kelly 'producer and abbess of a brothel'. As a woman from lower class origins her beautiful body was her biggest asset and she used it to gain access to aristocratic men. One such 'gentleman' Sir Harry Featherstonehaugh housed her in one of his cottages and in return she danced naked on the dining room table to entertain his guests. She then began an affair with Charles Greville during which time she became an artist's muse, being painted repeatedly by the artist George Romney as well as Joshua Reynolds. When Greville met and married a wealthy heiress she was shipped off to Naples where his

ageing uncle lived and worked as the British Envoy. The old man fell in love with her and much to the astonishment of his nephew married her making her the respectable Lady Hamilton.

After the success of the Battle of the Nile, Nelson returned home via Naples where Emma threw a huge party for him. They became besotted with each other and her husband seemed to tolerate the affair and even encourage it. The three dubbed themselves the 'tria juncto in uno'. They travelled slowly back to England, then lived openly together in Sir William's house. Emma gave birth to Nelson's daughter Horatia in 1801. That same year Nelson bought the rather dilapidated Merton Place and his rather strange extended family, consisting of his mistress, her mother, her husband and her daughter all lived happily together until his death at the Battle of Trafalgar in 1805.

Emma's extravagance and serious gambling habit led her into massive debt after her husband and her lover's deaths. She was not provided for despite Nelson's pleas on his deathbed for the government to care for her. She moved to France to escape her creditors and died in poverty in 1815.

The Wimbledon area is littered with reminders of its famous resident with roads, hospitals, pubs and schools named in honour of Lord Horatio Nelson commander of the victorious British fleet at the battle of Trafalgar.

The Nelson Arms commemorating another famous past resident RIGHT: Autumn leaves in Morden Hall Park

The fabulous virginia creeper
on Centre Court

LEFT AND BOTTOM RIGHT: Wimbledon Common
TOP RIGHT: Wimbledon Park golf course

LEFT: Autumn avenue
RIGHT: Riders enjoy the autumn colours
BELOW RIGHT: Fly-agaric, just one of the many
types of fungi to be found on the common in
the autumn

cannizaro

As well as having access to the common, residents of Wimbledon are lucky enough to have a beautiful park in their midst which is open to all. Once a private home, the house is now a luxury boutique hotel and the grounds are overseen by the local council who with the help of local volunteers maintain the garden which is full of specimen trees and shrubs. Because of its fine collection of rhododendrons, azalias and rare trees it was given Grade II listed garden status by English Heritage in 1987.

Originally known as Warren House it always had influential owners who socialized with the great and the good of their time. Thomas Walker, the first owner, was a great friend of Sir Robert Walpole, Britain's first Prime Minister, who was a regular visitor. Lyde Browne, the Governor of the Bank of England at the time, lived there in the mid 1700s. He is noteworthy for his huge art collection including many sculptures which he displayed in his house before selling most of his collection to Catherine the Great of Russia. She founded the famous Hermitage Museum in St Petersburg and the many art works from Wimbledon are still on display there today.

Next came Henry Dundas, Viscount Melville. He married a rich Scottish lady and when she committed adultery he divorced her. In those days all of a woman's wealth transferred to the husband on the day of the divorce so he became a very rich man. He remarried Lady Jane Hope. They moved into Warren House around 1785. He is responsible for the kitchen garden and the beautiful Lady Jane Wood which he planted in honour of his wife. He became Home Secretary in the government of Prime Minister William Pitt the Younger to whom he was a great friend. Pitt visited the house so frequently he had his own rooms within it. George III also was a regular guest, often coming for breakfast after surveying the troops at the military reviews held on Wimbledon Common. Dundas fell into disrepute when he was charged with corruption and was the last man to be impeached by the House of Lords. He was found not guilty of all charges but the events took their toll and he moved out of Warren House retreating from public life.

Francis Platemone, Count St Antonio, a penniless Italian Aristocrat and future Duke of Cannizaro then moved in with his rich and rather colourful wife and renamed the house 'Cannizaro'. At the time the duchess was described as 'a woman of rather amusing notoriety, who the world laughed with and at'. She was short, fat and uneducated but pretty

and great fun to be with. Their marriage was very rocky and the Duke became 'disgusted' with her and took off to Italy to live with his lover in Milan. He returned briefly only to be 'even more disgusted' by her and so left again. The second departure saw his wife chase him across Europe, but realizing that her attempts to get him back were futile she took up with an even more penniless, but young and virile Italian violinist whom she brought back to Cannizaro and lived with openly, causing a bit of gossip in leafy Wimbledon. Her legacy to Cannizaro was her love of music. It obsessed her every waking moment. She wasn't musical herself but put on recitals on Sundays and the house became famous for its musical evenings. From 1989 until recently, every summer saw the Cannizaro Festival where music was performed al fresco next to the Italian Garden.

In about 1879 Mrs Shulster and her daughter Adele moved in. Mrs Shulster became famous for her garden parties which were attended by royalty and famous writers such as Tennyson, Henry James and Oscar Wilde. Pastoral plays were performed in the grounds with Tennyson's *Becket* being a highlight. Adele, another comely lady, was particularly friendly with Oscar Wilde and he referred to her ironically as 'Miss Tiny'. She mustn't have minded too much as she gave him £1,000 when he was out on bail and he referred to her as 'a soul that renders the common air sweet'.

In 1900 when a Colonel Mitchel was living at the house a huge fire swept through the property all but destroying it. The fire exposed the inadequacies of the local fire brigade who did not have enough hoses to pump water from Rushmere

The splendid autumn colour spectrum on view in Cannizaro Park

Pond. Following this incident, the fire service was reformed and moved to new headquarters with better equipment. The house was almost completely rebuilt and the next significant residents were the Wilsons. Kenneth Wilson was responsible for much of the restoration of the gardens to their former glory and he planted many more specimen shrubs making the garden a special place again. After World War II the house and garden were sold to the Wimbledon Corporation and for some time the house was a nursing home and the garden was opened to the public. In 1987 the house was converted into a hotel with the gardens remaining in public ownership.

With the council being squeezed for money in the 1980s the gardens began to deteriorate and local residents set up the Friends of Cannizaro Park. Their membership has grown steadily and with money gained by fund raising events and council grants, improvements have brought the gardens back to pristine condition and it is now a pleasure to walk around this lovely urban park.

No. 1 Court in autumn

Heather, spiders webs and mist – a typical autumn morning on the common

early wimbledon

To be honest, history doesn't have much to say about Wimbledon until Tudor times. Unlike many places in the vicinity it has no mention in the Doomsday Book. At that time it was in the manor of Mortlake and came under the jurisdiction of the Archbishop of Canterbury, the Lord of the Manor. The manor of Mortlake was one of the largest in southern England and included in its borders Mortlake, East Sheen, Putney, Roehampton and Wimbledon.

In medieval times it went by the name of *'Wunemannedun'* suggesting a Saxon connection. In Saxon *'dun'* means 'place on its hill' and Wynmann could well have been a Saxon leader. So chances are that Wimbledon was first named by Mr Wynmann the Saxon who owned the house on the hill. More important at the time was Merton Abbey, located at the bottom of the hill where a large Sainsbury's supermarket now stands. It was a highly respected educational institute with former alumni including assassinated saint and Archbishop of Canterbury Thomas Becket, Nicholas Breakspeare the one and only Englishman who has managed to make it to the head of the Catholic Church as pope, and Walter de Merton who took his name from that of the Abbey and went on to become a rich and powerful man as Chancellor to both Henry III and Edward I. He was also responsible for the founding of Merton College, Oxford in 1264. The Abbey was closed in 1538 during the dissolution of the monasteries.

The Wimbledon plateau offers good views of the surrounding areas providing a favourable defensive position for defenders of the territory. The land is gravel on the surface resting on a layer of London clay. This was not good for the cultivation of crops but provided an adequate habitat for grazing animals and a plentiful supply of fuel.

Archeological finds indicate the presence of Iron Age man. Neolithic arrowheads and knives and Bronze Age round barrows have been found suggesting the area was used for both hunting and burying the dead. There are remnants of a large hill fort that now spreads across three fairways of the Royal Wimbledon golf course providing hazards for the golfers. It was probably built around 250 BC originally with a ditch and a 20ft rampart. This must have taken a considerable amount of time and effort to build but there is no evidence to suggest that it was ever more than a transitory refuge. It is known locally as 'Caesars Camp' and much to historians' annoyance referred to as a Roman fort. Caesar and his army never came anywhere near the fort. In fact it got its name from a Victorian mapmaker called Crunchley who decided to spice up his map by giving the fort a more exotic name so 'The Rounds' became 'Caesars Camp'.

In manorial times, the plateau was referred to as 'common land' – a large area of wasteland never brought into cultivation. In theory it was owned by the Lord of the Manor but because it was of little value, over centuries tenants gained certain 'rights of common'. Of little use to the Lord of the Manor but very valuable to his poor tenants. A tenant could graze oxen, sheep and pigs (with rings through their noses to stop them rooting up trees), and they could cut wood but the amount was carefully calculated in order to be

ABOVE: All that remains of the hill fort known as 'Caesars Camp'
LEFT: Bluegate gravel pit, Wimbledon Common

sustainable. They could collect 'thorns, brambles, ferns and furze' all year round and brushwood for fuel between 30 November and 25 March. They were also allowed to dig gravel and sand for their own use. These 'freebies' made a huge difference to the lives of the tenants. However, the manor records reveal that many tenants abused their rights and were fined for their misdemeanors. One such was John Veisy who in the 1460s grazed too many animals, failed to ring his pigs, and cut too much wood. Men of cloth were not exempt with the Chaplain of Wimbledon being fined 20 pence in 1467 for 'overburdening the common with ten cattle'. During the plague years the population of Wimbledon dropped by half and the ungrazed common reverted to waste or 'the wild land' as it was referred to locally.

The importance of Wimbledon changed considerably in the Tudor times when transport into London improved and the wealthy began to build large houses in the district.

'Capability' Brown's lake
in Wimbledon Park

windmills, woggles and watneys

Watneys Red Barrel beer became something of a cultural phenomenon in the 1960s and 70s, being mentioned in Monty Python sketches and period drama shows such as *Life on Mars*. The Watney family, part owners of the brewers Watney Mann which produced Red Barrel, had been Wimbledon residents for centuries. The family patriarch Daniel had leased land either side of Worple Way and successfully grazed cattle, grown corn and raised hops. His three sons all did well with William starting the family brewing business, Thomas managing Warren Farm near Beverley Brook and the youngest John taking over his father's estate and with the increasing profits building Rushmere House on Wimbledon Southside – now part of King's College School. John was a respected local businessman and a member of the local vestry (an early form of councillor). As well as land he owned many water mills on the River Wandle that were responsible for milling his corn.

In 1799 he applied to the manor court to enclose a piece of land on Wimbledon Common on which to build a windmill. The locals wanted to mill their own flour because the product they were being sold was not good enough. He didn't live long enough to see his project completed and it wasn't until almost twenty years later that the windmill was completed by the carpenter Charles Marsh. Its construction was unusual, known as a hollow post mill, this type of mill was almost unheard of in England although very common in Holland. The Marsh family operated the mill until 1864 when the Lord of the Manor Earl Spencer announced he was to enclose the common. This led to the Wimbledon and Putney Commons Act of 1871 which handed over the common to the public. The Marsh family sold the mill on the proviso that it could not be used as a working mill and therefore be in competition with their other mills. It instead was converted into housing for six families.

In those days the common was a wild place and the millers working in the windmill often combined their milling duties with those of keeping the peace. One of the responsibilities of these special constables was to prevent duels. Although strictly illegal by this time, dueling was still commonplace and Wimbledon Common was a popular haunt for such goings on. Miller Dann was witness to the duel between Lord Cardigan and Captain Tucket. Lord Cardigan survived and went on to lead his troops 'into the valley of death' at the Charge of the Light Brigade during the Crimean War. Another infamous duel involved the Prime Minister William Pitt the Younger who after insulting the Member of Parliament for Southwark, George Tierney, was challenged to 'pistols at dawn'. The two met and shots were fired but no one was hurt and they left the scene on good terms. Pitt's reputation however, was harmed with many people wondering whether he had lost his mind.

In 1908, Lord Robert Baden-Powell rented the Mill House and set to work writing his book *Scouting for Boys*. This book went onto sell 150 million copies making it the fourth bestselling book of the twentieth century. An army officer, he had already written several military books on military reconnaissance. This new book was written specifically for the youth market. Whilst writing it he took groups of boys camping on Brownsea Island to test out his ideas and this led directly to the formation of the Boy Scouts Movement. He was a controversial figure with much dispute as to his political and sexual leanings. The Boy Scout uniform originally had a swastika symbol on it. Whether this referred to its original Sanskrit meaning of 'good luck' or its much darker link with Hitler and fascism is not known but much debated. As is his sexuality with his biographers split as to whether his appreciation of the male form indicated his repressed homosexuality or not. Whatever the truth it has not affected the phenomenal success of his book and the Scout Movement which continues to flourish.

Today the windmill has been completely refurbished with the sails still turning and at weekends it is open to the public. The museum inside has exhibits on windmills, rural life and scouting and there is a café that is open all day all year round. It is especially popular with dog walkers who after a brisk early morning walk love to tuck into a hot bacon roll!

Exhibit in the Windmill Museum

The windmill on the common

Autumn – the season of
mists and mellow fruitfulness

A still, misty morning in Wimbledon Park

Early morning over Rushmere Pond

index